DATE DUE

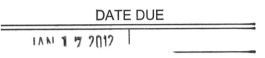

USAF SPECIAL TACTICS TEAMS

Jason Porterfield

rosen publishing's
rosen central®

New York

Published in 2009 by The Rosen Publishing Group, Inc.
29 East 21st Street, New York, NY 10010
www.rosenpublishing.com

Library of Congress Cataloging-in-Publication Data

Porterfield, Jason.
USAF special tactics teams / Jason Porterfield. — 1st ed.
    p.cm.—(Inside special operations)
Includes bibliographical references and index.
ISBN-13: 978-1-4042-1753-9 (library binding)
ISBN-13: 978-1-4358-5131-3 (pbk.)
6-pack ISBN-13: 978-1-4042-7862-2

1. United States—Air Force—Commando troops—Juvenile literature.
2. Special forces (Military science)—United States—Juvenile literature.
I. Title.
UG633.P658 2008
358.4—dc22

2007045390

Manufactured in Malaysia

On the cover: A member of a USAF Special Tactics team uses a satellite
phone during a training session on air support.

Contents

A member of a 62nd Special Tactics Squadron Combat Control team makes a demonstration jump alongside a United Kingdom Royal Air Force Combat Control team member. They are demonstrating a high altitude–low opening (HALO) jump.

Introduction

In the early days of the 2003 U.S. invasion of Iraq, a United States Air Force (USAF) Special Tactics team parachuted into Iraq under cover of darkness. Once on the ground, team members secured their unarmored vehicles and set out to find their targets. Within hours, they began pinpointing Iraqi tanks and calling in air strikes. They used their speedy all-terrain vehicles to stay out of range of enemy tanks as they targeted them with lasers. Over the course of just six hours, the air force destroyed thirty-five Iraqi tanks through the work of this Special Tactics team.

Armies have used special forces techniques such as this for thousands of years. By sending in small, mobile groups of soldiers trained to carry out specific pinpoint missions, armies can completely disrupt an enemy's activities. More important, attacks by special forces can destroy an enemy army's morale by taking its soldiers totally by surprise.

Since World War II, special operations forces—particulary those for the United States—have taken on increasingly prominent roles in conflicts around the world. The U.S. military has personnel committed to serving on bases across the globe. The use of special operations forces in armed conflicts and peacekeeping efforts allows the military to maintain some flexibility with its main forces.

Small, highly trained forces can often slip under enemy radar and pass into enemy territory undetected. Once there, they may attack targets that are only lightly guarded because no one expects an attack. Sophisticated technology enables special operations forces to work independently, giving them more room to operate in enemy territory. They can report on troop movements, mark targets, and rescue wounded servicepeople. Alternately, they also destroy enemy technology whenever possible, disrupting communications systems or radar.

Armed revolutionaries and terrorists around the world, from Southeast Asia to South America, gave the United States a reason to develop and hone its special forces. The military needed to be able to respond to guerrilla tactics and did so by creating some of the most highly trained special operations forces in the world.

In the future, the military may depend even more heavily on special operations forces. As warfare technology advances, someone on the ground needs to be able to set up the high-tech equipment and understand its workings. Forces made up of these tech-savvy warriors will likely be small, tough, and extremely mobile. Special operations forces such as Air Force Special Tactics teams will continue to shape the way wars are fought and the technology that is used to fight them.

1. Battlefield Airmen

Air Force Special Tactics teams exist as part of the Air Force Special Operations Command, its answer to the better-known Navy SEALs and Army Rangers. Special Tactics teams are trained for two primary battlefield missions: seizing enemy air bases, and recovering injured personnel from hostile territory. They are made up of combat controllers and pararescuers and are occasionally joined by special operations meteorologists (weather forecasters).

Today, the Air Force Special Operations Command consists of about 13,000 active, reserve, and National Guard personnel. About 300 of these are para-rescuers and combat controllers on active duty. More than 2,500 are permanently based overseas at bases in Germany, England, Japan, and other countries. The Air Force Special Operations Command operates 100 different aircraft, including helicopters and jets.

Staff Sgt. Jody Ball of the 10th Combat Weather Squadron provides security as another squadron member gathers data on cloud cover during a combat exercise.

The purpose of the Air Force Special Operations Command is to provide mobility, surgical-strike firepower, air support, and Special Tactics teams to the U.S. Special Operations Command. During conflicts, it works closely with army and navy special operations forces. Seven primary units currently make up the Air Force Special Operations Command: the 1st Special Operations Wing, the 27th Special Operations Wing, the 352nd Special Operations

Group, the 353rd Special Operations Group, the 720th Special Tactics Group, the U.S. Air Force Special Operations School, and the 18th Flight Test Squadron. Seven Air Force Reserve and Air National Guard units round out the Air Force Special Operations Command.

The 720th Special Tactics Group

The Air Force Special Tactics teams operate mostly out of the 720th Special Tactics Group, based at Hurlburt Field on Florida's Eglin Air Force Base. Units of the 720th are also scattered all over the United States, Europe, Asia, and the Pacific Islands. These include the 21st Special Tactics Squadron, the 22nd Special Tactics Squadron, the 24th Special Tactics Squadron, the 23rd Special Tactics Squadron, and the 321st Special Tactics Squadron, as well as the 10th Combat Weather Squadron.

Combat controllers, combat weather personnel, and pararescue forces are all part of the 720th. Their missions include air traffic control in combat situations, establishment of landing zones, close air support for air force strikes, and surgical strike missions with Spectre gunships. They also establish casualty collection points in combat zones to provide trauma care for wounded service personnel.

Combat Controllers

Combat controllers are among the most highly trained people in the armed forces. Before becoming members, they have to complete a thirty-five-week training course, as well as maintain an air traffic control qualification from the Federal Aviation Administration (FAA). Their specialty is air traffic control in combat situations and marking targets for light- or heat-seeking "smart" bombs and missiles. They can place a variety of forms of visible and infrared light on a target for the smart weapons to follow, lessening the chance of hitting an unintended target.

Combat controllers direct operations by special forces helicopters and the AC-130 Spectre gunships. Combat controllers often have to parachute directly into hostile situations with 100 pounds (45 kilograms) of equipment, secure the area, and immediately set up a temporary command center for guiding other forces into the area. They destroy enemy equipment and battle enemy forces using a wide variety of tactics, including ambushes and raids.

Combat controllers were first used in World War II, when the United States began using parachutes to insert troops behind enemy lines. Often, the paratroopers would end up widely scattered across the countryside, sometimes landing quite far from their targets. The army solved this problem by training

Paratroopers belonging to the 1st Allied Airborne Army land in Holland during World War II. At the time, the U.S. Air Force existed as a branch of the army.

a company of scouts called "Pathfinders," who were dropped into the area ahead of the main force. From the ground they used lights, flares, and smoke to signal to aircraft pilots and paratroopers that they were flying over the target. Pathfinders were particularly effective in the U.S. invasion of Italy and in guiding the 82nd and 101st Army Airborne Divisions during the D-Day invasion of June 6, 1944. When the U.S. Air Force was created in September 1947, the Pathfinders were renamed Combat Control Teams.

Today, combat controllers are paratrooper forces fully qualified to conduct combat operations on the ground to secure landing areas in active war zones. Their training includes demolition tactics for clearing obstacles from landing zones, and they often carry explosives. Combat controllers also learn how to set up and operate communications equipment and

Combat Weathermen

Combat Weather is another highly specialized branch of Air Force Special Operations. Combat weathermen are meteorologists specifically trained to forecast weather conditions on the battlefield, helping combat units decide when and how to stage an attack. Unlike the meteorologists who appear on television news programs, combat weathermen have to do more than collect data from various delicate instruments and analyze it within the comfort of a dry, indoor workstation. They have to base their predictions on their scientific knowledge of weather patterns and the conditions that they observe around them on the ground. Accuracy is key. If they are wrong, their predictions can endanger a combat mission.

Though they are part of the Air Force Special Operations Command, combat weathermen are usually embedded within other military units, such as the army's special operations units. In addition to being trained meteorologists, they are also trained warriors who actively participate in combat missions. If their predictions are wrong, they are exposed to the potentially deadly consequences along with the soldiers who make up the unit.

navigation gear so that they can direct air traffic in the combat area.

Pararescuers

Pararescuers are often called "PJs" from the days when they were known as pararescue jumpers. Their specialty is combat search-and-rescue, from which they derive their "That Others May Live" motto. Pararescuers are dropped directly into combat zones to find injured personnel, usually downed pilots or air crews. As trained paramedics, they must be able to move, think, and act quickly to stabilize and move out the injured, as they often

Satellite communications devices—like this one, being set up by a radio technician from the 347th Communications Squadron—are vital to Special Tactics operations.

do not have much time to perform their rescues. They are also trained in combat and are capable of fighting alongside many different military branches. Many times, they have to perform delicate medical care under enemy fire.

Pararescuers spring into action the minute they receive word of a downed plane or helicopter. They immediately draw upon the information available to them to develop a plan of action. They calculate the number of enemies in the target area, as well as the numbers and locations of any friendly forces. Pararescuers factor in terrain and ground cover in figuring out how much time they'll need to complete the rescue. If there are enemies nearby, they may have to make the rescue at night, under cover of darkness. If the terrain is particularly rugged, a daytime operation may be best, allowing for better visibility in negotiating tricky obstacles.

Once they've gathered all the information that they can, they assemble the equipment and forces that the mission requires. Nearly all pararescue missions are accompanied by a security force, called "shooters" by the tactical teams. Shooters are most likely to be other special forces personnel, such as Army Rangers, Army Special Forces, or Navy SEALS, depending on the situation.

2. The History of Air Force Special Operations

Of the five branches of the U.S. military, the air force is the youngest. Through WWII, the air force existed as part of the army. Its Special Forces component—what would eventually become the Air Force Special Operations Command—worked in high-threat areas under the guidance of the Office of Special Services (later renamed the Central Intelligence Agency, or CIA).

The 1st Air Commando Group

Air Force Special Operations Command was formally created in 1943, as the brainchild of U.S. Army general Henry "Hap" Arnold and British admiral Lord Louis Mountbatten. They created the 1st Air Commando Group in 1944 to provide assistance to British commando forces fighting in Asia.

General Henry "Hap" Arnold was commanding general of the U.S. Army Air Force from 1941 to 1945. Arnold strongly supported the creation of the U.S. Air Force as a separate branch of the military.

Fighter pilots Lieutenant Colonel Philip Cochran and Lieutenant John Alison were assigned the task of assembling the unit. Their guidelines were to make the unit self-sufficient, flexible, and highly motivated. They also had to be careful to maintain secrecy as they recruited fliers. While screening potential recruits, Cochran and Alison let them know that the operations they would be participating in would involve combat but told them little else. Because of the secrecy involved,

The P-51 Mustang was a single-seat fighter plane introduced during World War II. Fast and durable, it often accompanied Allied bombers on raids over Germany.

the 1st Air Commando Group's men adopted an unofficial uniform patch consisting of a black question mark on a white circle.

The 1st Air Commando Group's duties included supply drops and evacuations behind enemy lines. They became skilled in flying at low altitudes in their black-painted, modified B-25 bombers, P-51 Mustang and P-49 Thunderbolt fighters, and C-47 Dakota transport planes. Missions included everything from bombing raids to dropping off assault teams and spies, often at night, in bad weather and over rough terrain. Near the end of the war, they became the first combat group to use helicopters in combat. The 1st Air Commando Group's success quickly led to the formation of the 2nd and 3rd Air Commando Groups, which were also designated for service in Asia.

Meanwhile, in the European theater of World War II combat, the 801st Bombardment Group—called the "Carpetbaggers"—gathered information and dropped propaganda leaflets over hostile territory to convince the enemy to surrender. However, the 801st earned its reputation in the summer of 1944 as an elite unit through a series of daring rescues known collectively as the Halyard Mission. During the Halyard Mission, 801st crews and OSS operatives rescued more than four hundred air crews who had been shot down behind enemy lines.

The Korean War

The U.S. Air Force itself was established as a separate branch of the military in 1947. At the time, during the heightened nuclear tensions of the Cold War that was beginning to develop between the United States and Soviet Union, members of the air force leadership were focused on developing missiles and long-range bombers. They didn't consider any of the three Air Commando Groups necessary for future operations. All three were officially deactivated.

However, the Korean War (1950–1953) changed their minds. Following World War II, a civil war began in Korea between the country's Communist northern half and the democratic south. The United States became involved in the Korean War in 1950 as an ally to South Korea. That same year, the air force formed a new unit designed to perform covert operations in support of the CIA. The Air Resupply and Communications Service (ARCS) was formed in February 1951 under the direction of the Military Air Transport Service.

The ARCS used a wide variety of aircraft in its missions, most of it modified versions of outdated planes. The B-29 Superfortresses were particularly useful for dropping off special operations teams or agents. During WWII, they had been used for long-range bombing missions over Japan but had since been replaced by newer aircraft. The old Superfortresses were specially customized for their new missions. The bottom-rear gun turret on each plane was removed and replaced with a hatch. Special operations teams and intelligence agents called "rabbits" parachuted from these hatches from 500 feet (152 meters) or lower in order to avoid radar detection. These missions were often carried out at night in aircraft that had been painted black, making them harder to spot.

Detachment 2 was the name of another secret air force unit operating during the Korean War. Like the ARCS, Detachment 2 used aircraft that had been converted from their original purpose. The air crews of Detachment 2 rigged C-47 Dakota transport planes—usually used for carrying men or equipment—

to instead serve as bomber planes. Special racks and latch points were placed under the fuselage of each plane. These allowed each plane to carry two 75-gallon canisters of napalm, a highly flammable jelly-like substance made from gasoline. The C-47s flew low over the roads at night, burning North Korean supply convoys as they headed into South Korea. Detachment 2 also used their C-47s for psychological warfare, broadcasting messages in Korean to Communist forces and dropping leaflets urging them to surrender.

The Vietnam War

At the beginning of the 1960s, U.S. president John F. Kennedy pushed for the creation of new special operations units within all five branches of the military. Air force chief of staff General Curtis LeMay responded by creating the 4400th Combat Crew Training Squadron (CCTS) in 1961. When it started, the unit consisted of 350 men and officers, as well as thirty-two vintage propeller-driven aircraft, many of which had been used in World War II. They were to provide close air support to Special Forces operations behind enemy lines, as well as counterinsurgency training.

In November 1961, just months after its formation, the 4400th CCTS was deployed to Vietnam to train South Vietnamese pilots and give air support to Army Special Forces units in a

General Curtis LeMay, shown here with President John F. Kennedy, led the Strategic Air Command from 1949 to 1957. LeMay was air force chief of staff from 1961 until 1965.

mission called Operation Farm Gate. Thus, the 4400th CCTS became the first air force unit to participate in combat in the Vietnam War (1959–1975), using converted T-28 training planes to attack Communist North Vietnamese forces on the ground with bombs, machine guns, grenades, rockets, and napalm.

As the war in Vietnam intensified and the United States became more involved, General LeMay created the Special Air Warfare Center (SAWC) to help coordinate the air force's special operations units. The SAWC consisted of the revived 1st Air Commando Group, the 1st Air Combat Applications Group, and a combat support group.

Volunteers flocked to the SAWC, particularly to the 1st Air Commando Group, which grew to include six squadrons and more than three thousand personnel. In 1963, it was reclassified as an air force wing and renamed the 1st Air Commando Wing.

The Air Commando Squadron began revising old tactics and developing new ones for operations over Vietnam's varied terrain of jungles, mountains, valleys, and plains. The A-1E Skyraider became a common sight, as special operations personnel used them to search for and rescue downed pilots.

One of their most successful innovations was the conversion of the C-47 Dakota transport plane for pursuing North Vietnamese guerrilla forces. The aircraft were fitted with massive machine guns capable of firing enough bullets to fill every square inch of a football field within three seconds. These new gunships, as they were called, were also capable of dropping bombs and flares over targets. Their missions were to strike at night with their machine guns and flares to provide cover for other aircraft and U.S. Army Special Forces. They specifically protected Army Special Forces units, which were usually operating far from any other military support.

Newer C-130 Hercules transport planes were modified along similar lines as the C-47 gunships, but they also received advanced weapons and defense systems. Renamed the AC-130A "Spectre," the old "Hercs" were now assigned the task of destroying supply convoys and trucks. The Spectres became the military's most efficient truck destroyers. From 1969 to 1970, these planes damaged or destroyed an estimated 20,000 enemy trucks in Vietnam.

Air Force Special Operations forces began using helicopters extensively in rescue missions during the Vietnam War. Rescue

A helicopter gunner belonging to the 40th Aerospace Rescue and Recovery Squadron watches as another helicopter—belonging to the 21st Special Operations Squadron—flies by during a 1972 mission over Vietnam.

teams were formally organized in January 1966 as the Air Rescue and Recovery Services. The Air Rescue and Recovery Services quickly established themselves as elite rescuers. Using armed helicopters, they could hover over dense jungle and perform rescues with winches. They could also make landings on plains or even in swamps.

Reshaping Air Force Special Operations

The U.S. military began scaling back its forces and operations in Vietnam in the early 1970s, including those of the air force's special operations. Operations and personnel for the Air Force Special Operations forces were cut until June 1974, when their remaining members were placed in a single unit called the 834th Tactical Composite Wing. In 1975, the 834th was renamed the 1st Special Operations Wing, and by 1979, it was the only U.S. Air Force Special Operations force in existence.

That same year, the 1st Special Operations Wing was involved in a rescue mission in Iran. Its task, alongside special operations forces from the U.S. Army and Marines, was to rescue Americans being held hostage at the U.S. Embassy in the capital city of Tehran. The mission—called Operation Eagle Claw—required U.S. Air Force Special Operations pilots and Marine helicopter pilots to work together under cover of darkness with split-second timing. However, the Marines had not been trained to fly at night, and several helicopters got lost on the way to the staging area. The entire mission had to be called off because of the delay. As the helicopters returned to their base, one collided with an air force transport plane, killing eight servicemen.

Because most of the mistakes made in Operation Eagle Claw involved aircraft, much of the blame for the botched mission was placed on the air force's special forces. A review committee called the Holloway Commission convened to examine problems within all U.S. special operations forces. While the investigation took place, command of the 1st Special Operations Wing was transferred to the 23rd Air Force, which became one of the foremost special operations units.

As a result of the Holloway Commission's findings, the air force's special forces were once again reorganized as the 1st Special Operations Wing, this time bringing in the 8th Special Operations Squadron, the 16th Special Operations Squadron, and the 20th Special Operations Squadron, as well as some Air Force Reserve and National Guard forces. Their command would be at Hurlburt Field on the west end of Florida's Eglin Air Force Base.

Operation Urgent Fury

In October 1983, U.S. Air Force Special Operations managed to redeem itself for the mistakes made in Operation Eagle Claw. Operation Urgent Fury was a mission carried out by the 23rd Air Force on the island of Grenada, in the wake of an illegal coup and execution of the island's prime minister by military forces. The operation delivered U.S. Army Rangers to the Point Salines airport on Grenada, while Spectre gunships attacked Grenadan forces from the air.

Combat controllers belonging to the 23rd and 24th Special Tactics teams were air-dropped along with Army Rangers from a height of only 500 feet (152 meters). Along with their parachute gear, each combat controller carried about 90 pounds (41 kg) of equipment. They quickly secured the airport and set up a command center and communications network, coordinating landings for more special forces teams. Meanwhile, the 1st Special Operations Wing flew numerous missions throughout the country. During the entire operation, Air Force Special Operations suffered no casualties.

Following this dramatic military success, the air force began rebuilding its special operations forces. In 1987, the United States established the U.S. Special Operations Command to oversee all special forces operations.

Operation Just Cause

In 1989, the United States attacked Panama in order to capture Panamanian president General Manuel Noriega, who had interfered with his nation's elections and had been harassing U.S. troops stationed at the Panama Canal. U.S. Air Force Special Operations forces were heavily used in Operation Just Cause because of their ability to strike precisely and minimize the danger to Panamanian civilians.

Spectre gunships from the 16th Special Operations Squadron were sent into urban areas to attack Panamanian forces, while pararescuers were dropped in with Army Rangers. Combat controllers successfully set up air traffic operations at Paitilla Airport and disabled General Noriega's personal jet. Following the success of Operation Just Cause, the air force established the U.S. Air Force Special Operations Command in 1990, completing the rebuilding process for its special forces.

Recent Actions

In 1990, Iraqi president Saddam Hussein decided to invade Kuwait and take control of the smaller country's oil fields. Many nations around the world protested. A coalition of nations led by the United States began building up forces to invade Kuwait and drive the Iraqi army out.

On January 17, 1991, the U.S. Army attacked by destroying two Iraqi radar installations, beginning the first Gulf War. Guiding the army helicopters toward their targets were four Air Force Special Operations helicopters. Throughout the brief war, Air Force Special Operations would play a major part in targeting enemy forces, making supply drops, and conducting dangerous combat control missions. In the war's aftermath, they continued to play a role by dropping supplies to refugees in Iraq's northern territories.

Since then, Special Tactics teams and other special operations personnel have been deployed all over the world. Recently,

Special Tactics team members must be able to adapt to many different situations. Combat controllers working in mountainous Afghanistan during the 2001 strike against the Taliban used horses to cover the rugged terrain.

the United States has relied heavily on its special operations forces in overthrowing the Taliban regime in Afghanistan and continuing to pursue Taliban fighters (these are radical Islamist warriors aligned with terrorist mastermind Osama bin Laden). Special Tactics teams and special operations forces from the army chased Taliban fighters into Afghanistan's mountains, following the enemy over rough terrain into places a larger force would not be able to enter. They continue to play an active role in fighting against the Taliban in Afghanistan, as well as in the ongoing search for bin Laden.

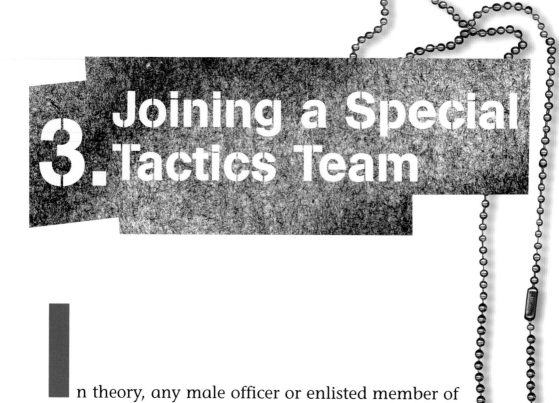

3. Joining a Special Tactics Team

In theory, any male officer or enlisted member of the air force can become a member of a Special Tactics team. Realistically, however, very few are actually qualified. Becoming a combat controller or pararescuer requires special training and knowledge, even before the Special Tactics training begins. Combat controllers have to be trained and certified in air traffic control, while pararescuers have to become trained paramedics capable of caring for the wounded and injured on the battlefield, in the heat of battle.

The PAST Test

Qualifying to become a member of a Special Tactics team starts with physical conditioning. Candidates must be fit enough to pass the Physical Abilities and Stamina Test (PAST) before training can begin. The PAST starts with a 25-meter (82 ft)

At Colorado's Air Force Academy, trainees must run an obstacle course that has a mud pit. Training also includes weapons training, tent inspections, and aerobic fitness tests.

underwater swim. The candidate fails if he breaks the surface even once. After the underwater swim, there is a five-minute rest period.

At the end of five minutes, the candidate has to complete a 1,000-meter (3,281 ft) surface swim within twenty-six minutes. If the candidate pauses during the swim, he fails. This swim is followed by a thirty-minute rest.

After the 1,000-meter swim and the rest period, the candidate must complete a 1.5-mile (2.4 kilometers) continuous run. The run cannot take longer than ten and a half minutes.

After a ten-minute cooldown period, the candidate begins four calisthenics challenges. He has to do eight chin-ups in sixty seconds, fifty sit-ups in two minutes, fifty push-ups in two minutes, and fifty flutter kicks. There are no breaks between any of those exercises.

Enlisted men who make it through the PAST test are then sent to the Indoctrination Course at Lackland Air Force Base in San Antonio, Texas. Officers, however, may need some physical retraining, since they are sometimes less physically fit than the younger enlisted candidates. They may have to do many of the things that they once did as enlisted men, including forced marches, navigating obstacle courses, distance runs, and swims. They also have to complete additional paperwork, including the soliciting of recommendations from superior officers and the writing of an essay explaining why they want to go through with the training. They must then appear before a review board of field officers, who select the top fifteen or twenty candidates out of every one hundred to proceed with the training.

The Indoctrination Course

At the Indoctrination Course, Special Tactics candidates face twelve weeks of training under the hot Texas sun. As they train, they are placed under constant evaluation by their trainers.

Indoctrination pushes the candidates beyond their physical and mental limits, guaranteeing that only the toughest will finish the training. Candidates often call the indoctrination course "Superman University."

The first two weeks of indoctrination consists of pure physical training. The physical tests that candidates completed for the PAST test are nothing compared to the challenges of indoctrination. Before they finish, candidates have to swim 4,000 meters (13,123 ft) with flippers in under eighty minutes and run 6 miles (9.7 km) in forty-two minutes. They must also do seventy-five push-ups, eighty sit-ups, thirteen pull-ups, fourteen chin-ups, and eighty-five flutter kicks in under two minutes for each exercise. In the third week comes a three-day trial called Motivation Week, consisting of constant physical trials at all hours of the day and night. Only about 10 percent of candidates make it through Motivation Week.

Motivation Week is then followed by several more weeks of tests and training. Water confidence tests—in which candidates must perform complex tasks in the water—are an important aspect of this training, with the goal of making candidates comfortable with working in such conditions. Combat training and marksmanship skills are sharpened in training sessions. Physiological training takes place in altitude and dive chambers, getting the candidates accustomed to working in different and unusual situations. Candidates also receive academic training to teach them how to analyze situations and give them a base of knowledge for situations that they might encounter.

The Pipeline

Once the candidates finish the Indoctrination Course, they enter specialty training, often called the "pipeline." The pipeline lasts between a year and a year and a half. By design, it transforms officers and enlisted men into highly skilled and motivated warriors. Because so many Special Tactics operations involve cooperation with the Navy SEALs, the pipeline training begins at the U.S. Army Combat Diving School in Key West, Florida. There, candidates learn how to use scuba gear to infiltrate targets.

These water exercises take place in the open ocean, day and night. Candidates in full scuba gear learn how to enter and leave a submarine while it is underwater. They also learn basic underwater demolition techniques, such as proper placement of explosives.

The next step in the pipeline is a trip to the U.S. Navy Underwater Egress Training at Florida's Pensacola Naval Base. Candidates are trained in the proper way to safely exit sinking or submerged aircraft. They learn how to use a Helicopter Emergency Egress Device System (HEEDS), which is a small scuba tank that holds a five-minute supply of air. Crews wear these tanks inside their survival vests in case they become trapped underwater.

A machine called the Helicopter Underwater Egress Trainer teaches candidates how to exit submerged helicopters. The candidate is strapped into a seat, just as if he were in a real helicopter. The machine then plunges this mock cockpit into 10 feet (3 m) of water, where it sinks. Candidates have to unfasten their seatbelts and exit while blindfolded to simulate darkened conditions under water. To get the most out of this training, instructors roll the mock helicopter cockpit so that it lands upside down. This provides the candidate with experience working in disorienting conditions.

Combat rescue officer candidates line up in the corner of a pool during a water confidence test. Being comfortable in the water is a key requirement for Special Tactics trainees.

Jump School

The underwater training is then followed by three weeks of basic airborne training at the U.S. Army's airborne training

A Special Tactics and Rescue Specialists team member makes a jump during a demonstration at Naval Air Station in Key West, Florida.

facility at Fort Benning, Georgia. When candidates graduate from this program, they are awarded the Silver Wings, which mark them as airborne warriors. They then go on to more advanced parachute training at the U.S. Army Military Freefall Parachutist School at Fort Bragg, Georgia.

There they learn the basics of military free-fall jumping and advanced techniques, such as high altitude–high opening parachute jumping. With these methods, they can infiltrate enemy territory undetected.

Part of their time at Fort Bragg is spent inside the free-fall simulator. This state-of-the-art, $5 million facility features an enclosed wind tunnel capable of creating wind speeds of up to 135 miles per hour (217 km per hour). The students are suspended in a column of air generated by the facility's fans and learn how to stabilize their bodies as though they were falling at a rate of 200 feet per second (61 m per second).

During free-fall parachute training, they also learn to deal with emergency situations, such as parachute malfunctions or entanglements. They learn procedures for cutting away their parachutes and opening their emergency parachutes quickly, since they would have little room for error when plummeting through the air.

After a week at Fort Bragg, candidates go to Yuma Proving Ground in Arizona. There, they practice jumping several times a week. They learn every type of jump from every altitude, sometimes jumping two or three times a day. They learn how to jump in any weather condition, with every type of equipment that would be available to them during an operation. At the end of five weeks, the candidates make sixteen free-fall jumps, including two daytime jumps and two nighttime jumps carrying oxygen and hundreds of pounds of field equipment.

Next, they head to Colville National Forest in Washington State and Kaniksu National Forest in Idaho for three weeks of wilderness training. They learn basic survival techniques, such as how to build shelters, find food and water, navigate with a compass, and signal to aircraft. They also go through a program called Survival, Evasion, Resistance and Escape, an intense program that teaches them how to survive physical and mental abuse in the event that they are captured by the enemy. Once this final part of the pipeline ends, candidates graduate and move on to concentrate on specialties.

Pararescue Training

After they complete their training in the pipeline, candidates interested in becoming pararescue jumpers attend the Special Operations Combat Medic Course at Fort Bragg. They spend twenty-four weeks receiving comprehensive medical training in the managing of trauma patients waiting to be evacuated. They also learn how to treat less serious injuries in the field. Candidates are assigned to four weeks of hands-on training in emergency rooms and hospitals, often in high-crime areas of New York City. There they learn firsthand how to treat gunshot and knife wounds, burns, and accident trauma.

Phase I of Combat Medic training teaches basic skills in emergency medicine. The second phase—which lasts seventeen weeks—teaches minor field surgery, pharmacology, combat trauma management, and advance airway treatment. At the end of Combat Medic training, candidates receive their Emergency Medical Personnel certifications and head to New Mexico's Kirtland Air Force Base for the ninety-day Pararescue Recovery Specialist Course.

The Pararescue Recovery Specialist Course is made up of three phases: the Ground Phase, the Medical Phase, and the Air Phase. The Ground Phase teaches candidates woodcraft and field craft—survival skills for hostile environments similar to what they learned in the pipeline. They learn about edible plants, how to trap wildlife and prepare food in the wild, and advanced land navigation.

The Medical Phase includes becoming used to the standard All-Purpose Lightweight Individual Carrying Equipment (ALICE) field pack, which is filled with medical supplies. Each ALICE pack must be arranged in exactly the same way, so that any PJ can work out of another PJ's kit without wasting time searching through it for a particular desired item. During training, the candidates become so familiar with these bags that they can operate out of them by blind touch alone. Near the end of the Medical Phase, candidates learn basic search-and-rescue techniques. Before graduating, they must plan, mount, and carry out a mock rescue mission and bring a survivor back alive.

The last phase of the Pararescue and Recovery Course is the Air Operations Phase. Candidates learn about many kinds of air force aircraft and how they work. They learn how to set up aerial searches and are taught how to insert themselves into rescue situations and bring back survivors. This includes using helicopter rope ladders, hoists, and rappelling techniques. They learn advanced methods of parachuting into water. During this phase of training, candidates make ten land jumps, two tree jumps into forests, and five scuba jumps into water. Four to six of these jumps take place at night. Once they finish this phase of the training, graduates are awarded their maroon berets and get to wear the air force crest "That Others May Live."

Combat Controller Training

Candidates for combat controller training begin by going to Keesler Air Force Base in Mississippi, where a fifteen-and-a-half-week class called the Combat Control Operator Course takes place. Teachers include both military and civilian air traffic controllers. Candidates learn basic flight rules, as well as radar approach procedures for landing, various aspects of tower and airport operations, and air traffic control. They also learn how to use air navigational aids, performance statistics for different aircraft, and weather forecasting. Once they complete this course, candidates take the Federal Aviation Administration's Control Tower Operator Exam.

Those who pass the exam go on to Combat Control School at North Carolina's Pope Air Force Base. They spend eighty-seven days learning combat tactics. These range from using communication and navigation equipment to demolition and fire support. They learn how to control air traffic in combat and how to prepare a landing zone. Training also stresses physical fitness. The candidates are put through rigorous daily exercises, including 6-mile (9.7 km) runs, long-distance swims, weight training, and quick marches with full packs.

Once they have learned the basics and proven themselves to be physically and mentally fit, the candidates go to Camp Mackall, North Carolina, to practice. They learn how to mark targets with laser pointers and receive further training in the preparation of landing zones. Near the end of this part of their training, they plan a mock mission. The mission calls for them to be inserted by parachute into the mock operation zone and carry out their orders under realistic

Members of the U.S. Air Force's 6th Special Operations Squadron provide cover fire during a staged ambush at Hurlburt Field. The operation was part of a nine-month-long Combat Aviation Advisor Mission Qualification Course.

conditions over ten days. At the end of this simulated mission, they march back to the Combat Control School fully equipped for combat and carrying 70 pounds (31.75 kg) of equipment in their rucksacks.

The candidates who complete this course may move on to conventional assignments, or they may complete more training to become qualified for Special Operations Tactical Air Control. They have to undergo Army Ranger training

Rubber Ducks

Air Force Special Tactics teams often find themselves working in or on the water and, therefore, undergo extensive training for aquatic missions. Team members call these missions "Rubber Ducks" because they require the team to use rubber Zodiac rafts. There are several different ways to deploy these rafts, and each method has a different nickname. In a Soft Duck operation, a fully inflated raft is dropped from a helicopter, with the team members dropping close behind. When they hit the water, they climb aboard the raft,

A Special Tactics team navigates a Zodiac inflatable raft during a "Rubber Duck" training mission at Hurlburt Field. The rafts are almost always inserted into combat from the air.

start the engine, and begin their mission. The same thing happens with a Hard Duck, except the raft's bottom is made of metal.

Kangaroo Ducks call for the fully inflated raft to be slung underneath a helicopter, like a baby kangaroo riding inside its mother's pouch. They are ready to go as soon as they hit the water. For Tether Ducks, on the other hand, the raft is deflated and rolled up inside the helicopter, meaning that the team has to inflate and load it with supplies before the mission begins.

and learn infantry-related skills so that when they become part of a Special Tactics team or work with Army Special Forces or Navy SEAL teams, they can keep up with the men around them.

Initial Familiarization

The final stage of training for combat controllers and para-rescuers is a course called Initial Familiarization. This one-month course brings combat controllers and pararescuers together to form teams. Through a series of intense exercises, these men bond together to form a lethal unit of Air Commandos.

Most of this training takes place at Eglin Air Force Base, aboard C-130 and AC-130 planes and Pave Low helicopters. The men learn how to operate the land vehicles used by Air Force Special Operations and how to load them into planes for transport. As a final test, the Special Tactics teams are attached to Army Ranger units. They work with the Rangers to plan, rehearse, and carry out a simulated airfield raid. Once they successfully complete this final test, they graduate and, after much excruciating and exhausting training, join the ranks of the Air Force Special Operations Command's Special Tactics Squadron.

4. Equipment, Gear, and Jump Tactics

The air force relies heavily on high-tech equipment for completing its missions. Aircraft constantly evolve, as does their navigation equipment and weapons systems. In most cases, the air force has developed specialty fixed-wing and rotary-wing aircraft for carrying out particular missions.

Many of the most advanced aircraft in the U.S. military are modified versions of very low-tech aircraft, particularly cargo planes. Throughout its entire history, the Air Force Special Operations

Command has converted simple planes to meet its strategic needs. Though the basic structure of the aircraft may be low-tech, the equipment inside makes them some of the most technologically advanced planes and helicopters in use throughout the military today.

The AC-130U Spectre

The AC-130U Spectre gunship is one of the most recognizable in the Air Force Special Operations arsenal. A fixed-wing aircraft, the Spectre originally evolved from the basic four-engine C-130 Hercules cargo plane, one of the military's most durable and reliable aircraft. Today's Spectres are designed and built exclusively for special operations, at a cost of $72 million per plane. Today, there are thirteen of these gunships operated by the 16th Special Operations Wing.

Spectres are mainly used for close air support, covering special forces units on the ground by attacking the enemy from the air. To this end, the gunships are packed with many different kinds of weapons. In the plane's nose is a Gatling cannon that fires 25-mm high-explosive incendiary rounds. This gun is capable of firing 1,800 rounds per minute from up to 12,000 feet—a distance of more than 2 miles (3.2 km).

Spectres are also equipped with a 40-mm Bofors gun that can fire explosive, incendiary shells or more conventional rounds.

The AC-130U Spectre was designed for close air support and armed reconnaissance. Among its many advanced weapons systems are radio and infrared sensors that identify friendly ground forces.

They also carry a massive 105-mm howitzer cannon, which is a field cannon modified to fire from a plane. The howitzers fire high-explosive and white phosphorous shells.

The Spectres don't fly as fast as most of the air force's jets, a fact that allows them to more easily control their fire and be more useful to forces on the ground. The weapons are directed from a Battle Management Center in the plane's fuselage. From here, the crew operates state-of-the-art sensors, navigation, and fire-control systems. Technicians can watch the battlefield from several monitors at once, using this information to direct the weapons systems. A tough composite armor made from silicon carbide and specially designed Spectra fiber protects the crew inside the Battle Management Center from enemy fire.

The targeting equipment inside a Spectre allows its crews to attack targets day or night and in bad weather, even if the target is shrouded in fog or heavy smoke. These systems include an infrared detection set, radar target detectors, and lasers for illuminating targets. The equipment is capable of detecting and engaging two targets at once, so that the Bofor gun and the howitzer can attack two separate targets at the same time.

The AC-130U Spectres have highly advanced navigation systems within the pilot's cabin. These include a global positioning system that allows the crew to pinpoint its exact location. The Spectres also come equipped with inertial navigation systems, which track the plane's velocity through special sensors that identify and note passing landmarks and coordinates.

Along with targeting and navigational equipment, Spectres are loaded with defensive systems to foil antiaircraft missiles. Flares act against radar and infrared guided missiles. To protect against heat-seeking missiles, the Spectre has a heat shield under its engines to disperse the extremely hot air it generates.

The MC-130E/H Combat Talon

Like the Spectre gunship, the MC-130E/H Combat Talon and Combat Talon II evolved from the Hercules cargo planes. They come equipped with radar designed to follow the terrain and help the plane avoid treacherous obstacles. They also feature equipment called forward looking infrared radar (FLIR). The FLIR uses infrared heat energy to create a picture for the pilot, so that he can "see" at night or in heavy fog.

Combat Talons are used to secretly deliver forces and equipment to hostile territory. They use global positioning and inertial navigation to make complicated air drops with great accuracy. Their navigation technology allows pilots to fly them at low altitudes and at night.

The Pave Low Helicopter

The MH-53J Pave Low III is the primary helicopter in the Air Force Special Operations Command arsenal. Pave Lows are built for low-level, long-range operations in hostile territory. They infiltrate, resupply, or extract special operations forces. They operate day and night in all kinds of weather. Their navigational systems include global positioning systems, forward looking radar, and inertial navigation systems.

At 92 feet (28 m) long and 25 feet (7.7 m) high, the Pave Lows are the largest and most powerful helicopters used by the air force. During the Vietnam War, the original Pave Lows were even nicknamed "Jolly Green Giants." Despite their size, they can fly at a rate of 200 miles per hour (321.9 km per hour) and are capable of lifting 20,000 pounds (9,072 kg). Pave Lows can haul thirty-eight fully equipped combat personnel or fourteen litters of equipment and supplies.

Other Vehicles

Once on the ground, Special Tactics teams sometimes make use of small vehicles to get around. One of the most versatile is the rescue all-terrain transport (RATT). The RATT is a lightweight yet sturdy four-wheel-drive, Jeep-like vehicle powered by a Porsche engine. The RATT was designed for driving over rugged terrain.

The MH-53J Pave Low III is the largest, most powerful helicopter serving the U.S. Air Force. It is also the most technologically advanced, featuring cutting-edge navigation and radar systems.

Often used in pararescue operations, RATTs can be fitted with up to six litters for carrying injured personnel, with enough remaining room for two or three pararescuers.

During the Korean War, Air Force Special Operations personnel called "rabbits" were often airdropped into enemy territory with radio sets and orders to scout the land. Pickup missions were often too risky or difficult, so the rabbits had to make it back to friendly territory on their own. The air force often helped them out by dropping them off with motorcycles, which were sturdy enough to make it over treacherous terrain. Today's Special Tactics teams still occasionally use motorcycles in their operations because of their speed and ruggedness. They sometimes use all-terrain vehicles (ATVs) for the same reasons.

Navigation and Communication Gear

Combat controllers are responsible for making sure that aircraft can take off and land in a particular area. They must set up and operate navigational equipment to help pilots find the landing site. Global positioning technology allows combat controllers to gather information from satellites and give their precise coordinates to friendly aircraft. The most commonly used positioning device is the Precise Lightweight GPS Receiver, nicknamed the "Rockwell Plugger" for the company that manufactures it. Once the coordinates are known, Tactical Air Navigation beacons broadcast a radio signal in all directions to tell incoming aircraft where to land or make a drop.

Special Operations Laser Acquisition Markers (SOFLAMs) give Special Tactics teams the ability to locate and designate enemy targets for destruction. When a combat controller marks a target with a SOFLAM, laser-guided bombs or missiles can lock onto it and blow it up. SOFLAMs are powerful enough that they can be used in broad daylight or in darkest night.

Special Tactics teams depend heavily on radios, which they use to communicate with outside forces, suppliers, and each other. Radio equipment comes in many shapes and sizes, from the umbrella-like satellite antennae of inter-team radios used to communicate with forces in the air to short-range handheld radio receivers carried by team members.

Jump Tactics

Since World War II, Air Force Special Operation forces have refined the art of dropping out of aircraft. They use parachutes, ropes, and hoists to get on the ground or into the water to support other special operations forces. Military free-fall operations are the most ideally suited for Special Tactics teams. They make their jumps anywhere from 43,000 feet (13,106 m) above the ground to just 5,000 feet (1,524 m), depending on the type of mission.

As the plane approaches the target area, team members put on their helmets and oxygen masks. This equipment makes it hard for them to hear each other, so they communicate through hand signals. Two minutes before jump time, a crew member called a jumpmaster signals for the team to stand up and move to the rear, where the hatch is located. Equipped with their parachutes, oxygen masks to keep them from passing

An air force combat controller uses his radio to call aircraft after successfully using tactical underwater breathing equipment to land on the Florida coast during a training exercise.

out, goggles to protect their eyes, and rucksacks filled with the equipment they'll need on the ground, they move to either the side jump door or the cargo ramp at the rear of the plane. When the aircraft reaches the coordinates for the target area, a green light goes on, and the airmen jump.

There are two different kinds of free-fall jumps: the high altitude–low opening (HALO) jump and the high altitude–high opening (HAHO) jump. The HALO jumps take place closer to the ground, with the drops occurring around 5,000 feet (1,524 m) above ground level and the parachutes opening at 3,500 feet (1,067 m). HALO jumps often take place at night, giving enemy forces less opportunity to spot the parachutes and capture the team. On the ground, the team members use their navigational skills to locate each other and meet up at a prearranged point.

HAHO jumps take place at extremely high altitudes and require that jumpers carry oxygen. Instead of free-falling before allowing their parachutes to open, HAHO jumpers open their parachutes immediately and use them to glide into the area they're infiltrating. They drop in formation, each member wearing a strobe on his helmet and communicating via radio in order to hold the formation. All Special Tactics team personnel are trained in both HALO and HAHO techniques.

Fast Ropes

Once, Special Tactics teams deployed from helicopters by rappelling down ropes. When they hit the ground, they had to waste precious seconds cutting their harnesses loose from the rope. Today, they still use rappelling techniques—mostly when dropping into urban areas or working in the mountains—but they have developed a new system for getting established on the ground quickly. This system is called the fast rope insertion system (FRIS).

The system uses ropes made of braided smaller ropes for added strength. The rope is rolled into a bag, and its end is clipped to the outside of the helicopter. Once the helicopter is over the target spot, the crew drops the rope. Instantly, before the end even hits the ground, the Special Tactics team members are sliding down it, hitting the ground safely within seconds. When everyone has touched down, the helicopter crew releases the rope by pulling out a pin, letting it drop to the ground.

Special Procedure Insertion/Extraction System (SPIES)

While the fast rope system can get Special Tactics teams on the ground quickly, the special procedure insertion/extraction system (SPIES) allows Pave Low helicopters to remove teams quickly when there is not an adequate or safe landing zone. A single rope is lowered from the helicopter with rings woven into it every 5 feet (1.5 m). There may be as many as eight rings on a single rope. The Special Tactics team members—all wearing harnesses with snap clips at the top—can clip themselves onto the rope and make their escape as the rope is raised.

This is the very essence of what the Air Force Special Tactics teams are all about—speed, danger, skill, cunning, courage, teamwork, lightning-fast operations, and daring escapes. They are the unsung heroes of any military mission, risking their own lives to save the lives of their brothers and sisters in uniform, creating secure areas where previously there was only chaos and enemy fire. Members of the Special Tactics teams are a rare breed. Soldiers, sailors, and pilots throughout the armed forces must feel greatly reassured to know that the Special Tactics teams have their back.

Glossary

convoy A group of military vehicles traveling together.

fuselage The central part of an airplane, designed to accommodate crew, passengers, or cargo.

global positioning system (GPS) A network of satellites that can provide precise geographic locations.

gunship A type of heavily armed aircraft, designed for intense fighting with ground forces.

howitzer A type of large, short-range cannon that fires at high elevations.

incendiary Capable of starting fires.

indoctrination A period of training in which thoughts or beliefs are imposed on a person.

infrared Having or employing wavelengths outside of the visual spectrum.

radar A device that picks up on microwave radiation to locate and measure distant objects.

rappel To descend to a lower height using a system of ropes and harnesses.

scuba Acronym meaning "self-contained underwater breathing apparatus."

special operations Small-scale military missions often carried out in secret or capitalizing on the element of surprise.

squadron An air force unit smaller than a group but larger than a flight.

tactic A plan for reaching a goal; a strategy for achieving a certain end.

white phosphorous A glowing chemical that burns when exposed to water and that can cause chemical burns upon contact with the skin.

winch A crank with a line attached to it, designed for lifting or pulling heavy objects.

For More Information

Air Force Special Operations Command

AFSOC/Public Affairs

229 Cody Avenue, Suite 103

Hurlburt Field, FL 32544

(850) 884-5515

Web site: http://www2.afsoc.af.mil

This is the headquarters for Air Force Special Operations.

Central Intelligence Agency (CIA)

Office of Public Affairs

Washington, DC 20505

(703) 482-0623

Web site: https://www.cia.gov

The CIA often works with Special Forces.

National Museum of the U.S. Air Force
1100 Spaatz Street
Wright-Patterson AFB, OH 45433
(937) 255-3286
Web site: http://www.nationalmuseum.af.mil
This museum documents the history of the U.S. Air Force.

U.S. Special Forces Command
HQ USSOCOM
ATTN: SOCS-PA
7701 Tampa Point Boulevard
MacDill AFB, FL 33621-5323
(813) 826-4600
Web site: http://www.socom.mil
Headquarters for the U.S. Special Forces Command.

Web Sites

Due to the changing nature of Internet links, Rosen Publishing has developed an online list of Web sites related to the subject of this book. This site is updated regularly. Please use this link to access the list:

http://www.rosenlinks.com/iso/ustt

For Further Reading

Alagna, Magdalena. *Life Inside the Air Force Academy.* New York, NY: Children's Press, 2002.

Axelrod, Alan. *Encyclopedia of the American Armed Forces.* New York, NY: Facts On File, 2005.

Camelo, Wilson. *The U.S. Air Force and Military Careers.* Berkeley Heights, NJ: Enslow Publishers, Inc., 2006.

Green, William, and Gordon Swanborough. *The Great Book of Fighters: An Illustrated Encyclopedia of Every Fighter Built and Flown.* Osceola, WI: MBI Publishing Company, 2001.

Hopkins, Ellen. *United States Air Force.* Chicago, IL: Heinemann Library, 2004.

Langley, Wanda. *The Air Force in Action.* Berkeley Heights, NJ: Enslow Publishers, Inc., 2001.

McCarthy, James P., ed. *The Air Force.* Andrews AFB, MD: Air Force Historical Foundation, 2002.

Roberts, Jeremy. *U.S. Air Force Special Operations.* Minneapolis, MN: Lerner Publications Company, 2005.

Bibliography

Air Force Special Operations Command. "Combat Controllers Fact
Sheet." Retrieved October 2007 (http://www2.afsoc.af.mil/
library/factsheets/factsheet.asp?id=201).

Air Force Special Operations Command. "Pararescue Fact Sheet."
Retrieved October 2007 (http://www2.afsoc.af.mil/library/
factsheets/factsheet.asp?id=217).

Air Force Special Operations Command. "Special Operations
Weather Fact Sheet." Retrieved October 2007 (http://www2.
afsoc.af.mil/library/factsheets/factsheet.asp?id=222).

Brehm, Jack, and Pete Nelson. *That Others May Live: The True Story
of a PJ, a Member of America's Most Daring Rescue Force.* New
York, NY: Crown Publishers, 2000.

Cerasini, Marc. *The Complete Idiot's Guide to the U.S. Special Ops
Forces.* Indianapolis, IN: Alpha Books, 2002.

Drury, Bob. *The Rescue Season: The Heroic Story of Parajumpers on the Edge of the World.* New York, NY: Simon & Schuster: 2001.

Hirsh, Michael. *None Braver: U.S. Air Force Pararescuemen in the War on Terrorism.* New York, NY: New American Library, 2003.

Kelly, Orr. *From a Dark Sky: The Story of U.S. Air Force Special Operations.* Novato, CA: Presidio Press, 1996.

Leebaert, Derek. *To Dare and to Conquer: Special Operations and the Destiny of Nations, from Achilles to Al-Qaeda.* New York, NY: Little, Brown and Company, 2006.

Pushies, Fred J. *U.S. Air Force Special Ops.* Osceola, WI: MBI Publishing Company, 2000.

Schreitmueller, Ginger. "Combat Weathermen, Move, Shoot, Communicate with Army SOF." Air Forces Special Forces Command Public Affairs, October 31, 2000. Retrieved October 2007 (http://www.specialtactics.com/weatherarticle.shtml).

Vanden Brook, Tom. "Precision Technology Helps Combat Troops Pinpoint Enemy." USAToday.com, August 27, 2006. Retrieved October 2007 (http://www.usatoday.com/tech/news/techinnovations/2006-08-27-rover-tech_x.htm).

Index

About the Author

Jason Porterfield has written more than twenty books for Rosen, on topics ranging from pirates to steroids. While researching this topic, he was struck by the strength and dedication required to join the Air Force Special Forces. The research also made him determined to try skydiving.

Photo Credits

Cover, p. 1 © Leif Skoogfors/Corbis; cover (inset), pp. 1 (inset), 4, 9, 13, 14, 24, 31, 35, 36, 41, 42, 46, 49, 52 Department of Defense; p. 12 © Getty Images; p. 17 © Time-Life Pictures/Getty Images; p. 18 Library of Congress Prints and Photographs Division; p. 22 © Bettmann/Corbis; p. 29 © AP Photos.

Designer: Les Kanturek; **Editor:** Peter Herman
Photo Researcher: Marty Levick